Siamese Cats as Pets

A Complete Ultimate Guide

Facts & Information, where to buy, health, diet, lifespan, types, breeding, care and more!

By Lolly Brown

D1384209

Copyrights and Trademarks

Disclaimer and Legal Notice

Foreword

The first distinctly recognized breed of Asian cats to come out of the Orient is the Siamese cat from the far, exotic lands of Siam, presently known as Thailand. The rich root of the Siamese cat goes far back to the Wichianmat (Thai cat) landrace which is one of the diverse varieties of cats native to Thailand.

The Siamese cat, with its playful and friendly demeanor, soon became one of the most sought after cat breeds in North America and Europe in the 20th century.

After years of thoughtful refinement, the Siamese we now know and love is distinguished by its hypnotizing blue, almond-shaped eyes which are set on its elegantly triangular head with its comically large ears sitting atop. It carries itself on an elongated body which is muscular and slender as well as agile and graceful.

Its coat coloration is a unique pale with relatively darker extremities on its face, ears, paws and tail. A cat that is dressed to the nines, the Siamese cat holds distinct characteristics that make it appear like it were ready to sashay and impress at a fancy masquerade ball.

Its chatty nature makes for great company on any given day and will keep you and the rest of the family engaged and involved.

This book aims to give you the low-down on what to expect when considering adding a Siamese cat as loving companion to your home. Find out what its needs are; what characteristics it has and what it takes to give it the care it requires.

Table of Contents

Chapter One: Introduction..1

    Glossary of Cat Terms 7

Chapter Two: Siamese Cats in Focus....................................15

    Interesting Facts about the Siamese cat 16

    A Summary of Facts about the Siamese cat....................18

    The Siamese cat Breed History 20

    The Oriental Siamese Reaches Western Shores.............21

    The Siamese Introduced to the Western Public 22

    Informative Tidbits about the Siamese Cat 25

    The Traditional Siamese vs. the Modern Siamese 27

Chapter Three: Siamese Cat Requirements 29

    Should You Opt for More Than One Siamese cat?........30

    Cats and Humans 31

    Do Siamese Cats Get Along Well with Other Pets? 33

    What does it Cost to take in a Siamese cat?....................34

        Initial Costs 35

    What Are the Pros and Cons of Owning a Siamese cat? .36

        Pros of Owning a Siamese Cat................................36

Chapter Four: Acquiring Your Very Own Siamese Cats....39

    Where Should You Look to Acquire a Siamese Cat? 40

Things to Remember When Looking for a Reputable Breeder..41

Adopt a Siamese cat from a Rescue 44

List of Websites of Breeders and Rescue Adoption 45

Another Bit of Siamese cat Trivia.....................................47

Selecting a Healthy Siamese cat 48

How to Feline-Proof Your Home 53

Chapter Five: Living with Your Siamese Cats 59

Habitat and Activity Needs for Siamese Cats 60

Keeping Your Siamese cat Healthy and Fit 62

Equipment You Need to Supply for Your Siamese cat....63

The Personality of a Siamese Cat 66

Chapter Six: Nutritional Needs of Siamese Cats 71

The Nutritional Needs of Siamese Cats 72

Raw Feeding or Commercial Food 73

Chapter Seven: Showing Your Siamese Cat 77

CFA Breeding Standards...84

The Thai Cat - TICA Standard 94

Chapter Eight: Breeding Your Siamese Cats 97

Siamese Cat Breeding Information 98

Chapter Nine: Keeping Your Siamese Cat Healthy 103

Siamese Cat Care Sheet 109

Basic Siamese Cat Information 111

Basic Nutritional Information.. 112

Breeding Information.. 113

Index... 115

Photo Credits 119

References.. 121

Chapter One: Introduction

Cats, in general, are known to be independent beasts and are said to be aloof. It is no wonder that countless individuals who are just as independent choose to raise cats and keep them as companions.

Siamese cats are generally, if not collectively, people-cats and love being around other pets that are as equally friendly to them. Discovered to be highly trainable, these felines have tugged at the heartstrings of many feline lovers and has changed the mind of many a canine guardians.

These traits are what set the Siamese cat apart from most other cat breeds. It's open, receptive and welcoming personality, as well as its tendency to seek out the companionship of humans, other felines and even select cat-friendly canines has made the Siamese cat a popular choice for big or small families with existing pets. They have come to understand that the "smartly-dressed" Siamese is not at all the haughty feline it is often times portrayed on TV and in films and that it thrives best in a loving household.

Its sociable demeanor and its penchant to "chat up" its humans have endeared it to many Siamese guardians and caregivers over time and it continues to garner popularity to this day. The Siamese cat will have a lot to say and will want you to pay mind when it speaks to you. It can be relentless in trying to gain your attention, so it is important to note that the Siamese is happiest around your presence.

When you decide to commit to the long term responsibility of owning a pet, you will need to consider the long haul and everything in between of being guardian to one. This will mean that you should be ready to give it the care it needs. It entails providing for and supplying it with everything that it would require maintaining sound health, both mentally and physically.

You shall have to factor in the expenses of its health and upkeep into your monthly expense. Regardless of breed, all felines require taking care of with utmost consideration and care, from medical visits, in order to monitor its health and well-being, to grooming and nutrition, as well its daily nutritional needs. These will all be under your watch and the feline will greatly be dependent on you and other caregivers who will share responsibility for it.

Siamese cats are pretty popular because of their unique look and easy-going nature. Count yourself lucky if you are given the opportunity to care for one through adoption as they can cost a pretty penny should you want to buy one. Not only are they sought after for their unique appearance and jovial personality, they are also popular because of their penchant to make friends with each member of the family and more so because of how they loyally attach themselves to one person in particular.

Keep in mind that caring for a Siamese requires much more than your initial investment during the acquisition of one. It will take a little bit of time, lots of loving care and a considerable amount of effort on your end to integrate your new Siamese into the family fold.

Whatever breed of cat or dog you may decide to choose, whenever adding a furry pal to the family dynamics, it will require your commitment, a good portion of your time and lots and lots of loving patience.

The Siamese cat is a pretty sociable feline who languishes on gentle play therefore they blend into families with little tots well. If your household comes ready with other pets, whether they be feline-friendly dogs and/or other cats, you would be pleased to discover that the Siamese, with patient introduction will easily get on with your other furry pals.

Because of its unique look and traits of being friendly and loyal, it is highly recommended to keep your Siamese buddy as an indoor pet. This measure of safety is strongly suggested to keep your Siamese cat safe from unwarranted attacks from larger animals. Keeping your Siamese indoors also decreases the chances of your Siamese being infected with illnesses they may contract from coming into contact with diseased or infected animals, feral and strays. This measure also wards off would be cat - nappers from running off with your furry buddy. After all, you have to remember that it's beautifully unique look makes it an eye-catching animal that many would love to have for their own.

It is imperative that you get to know and learn about the type of cat you will be incorporating into your household when thinking about a pet for yourself and family.

The information within this book hopes to enlighten you in finding out more about the Siamese cat. It shall unveil informative tips, and useful information that will empower you to take better care of your feline pal.

This book also aims to reveal the many benefits of taking in a Siamese cat. A loyal feline who thrives best in your loving company and who will keep you entertained and engaged for many days to comes. You will discover that its tendency to gravitate toward humans is innate and it is one that does not do too well when left alone for extended periods of time. You will also discover that, despite its lofty appearance, it is one friendly feline who manages to attach itself to one particular person and develops strong bonds with them.

The Siamese cat is at its finest when languishing about with its human guardians and dotes on pockets of moments when it can just relax and catch up with you as you sit to enjoy a good book or your favorite TV show. It is somewhat of a busy-body who will follow you around your home, piping in and vocalizing its thoughts on how you carry about chores and tasks around the house. It will try to "help" out on occasion and give you loud "suggestions" on how to go about the work you do. It will not want to be left alone and will make its presence felt and known when you are around.

Having read this far into this book would mean that you are perhaps one of the countless many who are in strong consideration of adopting or acquiring a Siamese cat. If you are in the market for a buddy who will chime in and speak its mind, if you are seeking the companionship of a feline who absolutely loves attention and pays you just as much mind as it needs, then you have come to the right place.

As you read further, you will find out more about the traits and characteristics of this exotic looking feline. The succeeding information within targets to, hopefully, help you come closer to a decision on bringing home a Siamese or two for your family to love.

Glossary of Cat Terms

Abundism – Referring to a cat that has markings more prolific than is normal.

Acariasis – A type of mite infection.

ACF – Australian Cat Federation

Affix – A cattery name that follows the cat's registered name; cattery owner, not the breeder of the cat.

Agouti – A type of natural coloring pattern in which individual hairs have bands of light and dark coloring.

Ailurophile – A person who loves cats.

Albino – A type of genetic mutation which results in little to no pigmentation, in the eyes, skin, and coat.

Allbreed – Referring to a show that accepts all breeds or a judge who is qualified to judge all breeds.

Alley Cat – A non-pedigreed cat.

Alter – A desexed cat; a male cat that has been neutered or a female that has been spayed.

Amino Acid – The building blocks of protein; there are 22 types for cats, 11 of which can be synthesized and 11 which must come from the diet (see essential amino acid).

Anestrus – The period between estrus cycles in a female cat.

Any Other Variety (AOV) – A registered cat that doesn't conform to the breed standard.

ASH – American Shorthair, a breed of cat.

Back Cross – A type of breeding in which the offspring is mated back to the parent.

Balance – Referring to the cat's structure; proportional in accordance with the breed standard.

Barring – Describing the tabby's striped markings.

Base Color – The color of the coat.

Bicolor – A cat with patched color and white.

Blaze – A white coloring on the face, usually in the shape of an inverted V.

Bloodline – The pedigree of the cat.

Brindle – A type of coloring, a brownish or tawny coat with streaks of another color.

Castration – The surgical removal of a male cat's testicles.

Cat Show – An event where cats are shown and judged.

Cattery – A registered cat breeder; also, a place where cats may be boarded.

CFA – The Cat Fanciers Association.

Cobby – A compact body type.

Colony – A group of cats living wild outside.

Color Point – A type of coat pattern that is controlled by color point alleles; pigmentation on the tail, legs, face, and ears with an ivory or white coat.

Colostrum – The first milk produced by a lactating female; contains vital nutrients and antibodies.

Conformation – The degree to which a pedigreed cat adheres to the breed standard.

Cross Breed – The offspring produced by mating two distinct breeds.

Dam – The female parent.

Declawing – The surgical removal of the cat's claw and first toe joint.

Developed Breed – A breed that was developed through selective breeding and crossing with established breeds.

Down Hairs – The short, fine hairs closest to the body which keep the cat warm.

DSH – Domestic Shorthair.

Estrus – The reproductive cycle in female cats during which she becomes fertile and receptive to mating.

Fading Kitten Syndrome – Kittens that die within the first two weeks after birth; the cause is generally unknown.

Feral – A wild, untamed cat of domestic descent.

Gestation – Pregnancy; the period during which the fetuses develop in the female's uterus.

Guard Hairs – Coarse, outer hairs on the coat.

Harlequin – A type of coloring in which there are van markings of any color with the addition of small patches of the same color on the legs and body.

Inbreeding – The breeding of related cats within a closed group or breed.

Kibble – Another name for dry cat food.

Lilac – A type of coat color that is pale pinkish-gray.

Line – The pedigree of ancestors; family tree.

Litter – The name given to a group of kittens born at the same time from a single female.

Mask – A type of coloring seen on the face in some breeds.

Matts – Knots or tangles in the cat's fur.

Mittens – White markings on the feet of a cat.

Moggie – Another name for a mixed breed cat.

Mutation – A change in the DNA of a cell.

Muzzle – The nose and jaws of an animal.

Natural Breed – A breed that developed without selective breeding or the assistance of humans.

Neutering – Desexing a male cat.

Open Show – A show in which spectators are allowed to view the judging.

Pads – The thick skin on the bottom of the feet.

Particolor – A type of coloration in which there are markings of two or more distinct colors.

Patched – A type of coloration in which there is any solid color, tabby, or tortoiseshell color plus white.

Pedigree – A purebred cat; the cat's papers showing its family history.

Pet Quality – A cat that is not deemed of high enough standard to be shown or bred.

Piebald – A cat with white patches of fur.

Points – Also color points; markings of contrasting color on the face, ears, legs, and tail.

Pricked – Referring to ears that sit upright.

Purebred – A pedigreed cat.

Queen – An intact female cat.

Roman Nose – A type of nose shape with a bump or arch.

Scruff – The loose skin on the back of a cat's neck.

Selective Breeding – A method of modifying or improving a breed by choosing cats with desirable traits.

Senior – A cat that is more than 5 but less than 7 years old.

Sire – The male parent of a cat.

Solid – Also self; a cat with a single coat color.

Spay – Desexing a female cat.

Stud – An intact male cat.

Tabby – A type of coat pattern consisting of a contrasting color over a ground color.

Tom Cat – An intact male cat.

Tortoiseshell – A type of coat pattern consisting of a mosaic of red or cream and another base color.

Tri-Color – A type of coat pattern consisting of three distinct colors in the coat.

Tuxedo – A black and white cat.

Unaltered – A cat that has not been desexed.

Chapter Two: Siamese Cats in Focus

The highly intelligent, smartly-dressed and elegant looking Siamese cat is a breed of feline which is recognized by some of the best known and well-trusted cat associations in the United States and around the world. Cat associations like the Cat Fanciers' Association (CFA), The International Cat Association (TICA), the Cat Aficionado Association (CAA) and the American Cat Fanciers Association (ACFA) not only recognizes its one-of-kind appearance which sets it apart from most felines, these associations also recognize and laud the Siamese for its valuable contribution in the creation and development of other feline breeds that we enjoy today.

Earlier in this book you read a little bit about how Siamese cats tend to gravitate towards humans and depend on them for their upkeep, maintenance and care. As you continue to pursue information within these pages you will discover more about it traits and characteristics, medical conditions it can be prone to as well as properly caring for them. Details here and that follow aim to reveal more about this mysterious looking feline and what it would take for you to adopt, acquire or take in one or more of these lovable cats.

Interesting Facts about the Siamese cat

All Siamese cats of today can trace their lineage back to the original cats shipped in from the exotic lands of Thailand (known as Siam, once upon a time). You will discover that the first recorded Siamese cat to reach Western shores was given the moniker "Siam" taken from the name of the land from which it hailed. You'll get to know more about its beginnings in Western shores and how it was developed to the present day feline we have come to recognize and adore.

Siamese cats have been playing a vital role in the production of many other breeds that are present today in our modern society. It has played an important role in the initial breeding stages of some of the best loved cats we see today and continues to play a role of importance in the production of some of the most sought after felines that people seek.

With its close to the skin coat, the Siamese cat is certainly not a cat that requires too much grooming maintenance - save for the occasional brushing of teeth and coat and regular nail trimming, the Siamese requires very little. Keeping it on a grooming schedule though is a strong recommendation as this will help the cat follow a regular discipline of keeping and staying clean, thereby maintaining overall good health.

They integrate easily with loving support and gentle introduction with other felines and cat-friendly canines. If you are in strong consideration of welcoming a pet into your household, the Siamese cat is definitely one feline you would want to consider given its inclination to make friends easily. Its loyalty is unmatched and you will soon realize that the Siamese will possibly favor one particular person in the family but will get along with everyone.

A Summary of Facts about the Siamese cat

Pedigree: Cat Fanciers' Association

Group: Siamese Cat

Breed Size: Medium,

Height: 10-15 inches (25-38 cm) tall

Weight: 8-12 lbs. for females and 8 lbs. for males

Coat Texture: short

Color: **Lilac point**, a glacial white body with frosty pinky-gray points and lavender-pink nose leather and paw pads; **Blue point**, a bluish-white body with deep blue points and slate-colored nose leather and paw pads; **Chocolate point**, an ivory body with milk chocolate-colored points and cinnamon-pink nose leather and paw pads; and **Seal Point**, a pale fawn to cream body with deep seal brown points and deep brown nose leather and paw pads

Eyes: expressively close-set almond-shaped eyes that are a vivid, deep blue.

Ears: set at a wide base the Siamese ears are big and sticks up from the sides of its head and forms an imaginary triangular shape.

Tail: its tail, long and thin, bearing the color point of the cat, tapers to an elegant point.

Temperament: it needs lots of attention, is a vocal chatterbox and loves being around and interacting with its caregivers.

Strangers: it is a sociable feline; hence, it is strongly advised that you keep your Siamese as an indoor pet to fend of cat-nappers.

Other Pets: with the guardians patient integration it easily adapts to other feline friendly pets you may own

Training: is very trainable and easily adapts to humans who handle them with care

Exercise Needs: lively and frequent exercise is highly encouraged for the Siamese cat to keep it agile and limber.

Health Conditions: Siamese cats are prone to Amyloidosis, asthma and aortic stenosis.

Lifespan: typical average lifespan is 11-15 years

The Siamese cat Breed History

This docile yet notoriously frisky feline derived its name from the shores of its exotic, far flung origins of ancient Siam (presently known as Thailand).

It has been noted that the Siamese cat was one of several felines which served as great inspiration during the writing of the ancient manuscripts titled "Tamra Maew" or Cat Poems. The Siamese cat has been largely described in these texts and had been an inspirational muse for this great book of poems.

It is well known for its very distinct point color markings which give it an air of hushed elegance and sophistication and makes it very different from other feline breeds.

The Siamese cat looks like it got dressed up for a fancy masquerade ball in pale evening wear made chic by dark accessories. It peeps at you through its almond-shaped, tanzanite-blue eyes, brimming with expressive intelligence, and a childlike playfulness of quiet mischief.

It's interesting to know how far the Siamese cat managed to travel from the far shores of its native Thailand

(Siam) and how it landed on Western shores where it is now affectionately cherished and sought after for companionship by many cat fanciers and feline aficionados.

The Oriental Siamese Reaches Western Shores

The 19th American President, Rutherford Hayes, in 1878, was the first recorded recipient of a Siamese cat in the US. He, along with his wife Lucy, was the first people in the United States documented to have been guardians to the feline from the Orient. The Presidential Siamese cat was lovingly named "Siam", and was a gift to then President Hayes from US Consul David B. Sickels who was stationed in Bangkok then.

Later in 1884, Edward Blencowe Gould, the British Consul General of Bangkok brought home to his native Britain a pair of breeding cats he named Mia and Pho. He gifted his sister, Lilian Jane Gould with the stunning pair. It was Lilian Jane Gould who went on to cofound, in 1901, the first Siamese Cat Club.

A year later, in 1885, the United Kingdom Siameses Pho and Mia produced three adorable Siamese kittens which were named, Kalahom, Khromata and Duen Ngai. The three kittens along with their parents were brought to and shown at the London Crystal Palace Show. These families of unusual-looking felines with their deep blue eyes and unique colour pattern of point coloring have elicited great interest from the attendees of the show.

The Siamese Introduced to the Western Public

Their one-of-a-kind appearance and their uniquely distinct behavior drew droves of onlookers and they were an instant hit at the event. Sadly, all three kittens met their demise soon after the showing. The cause of their deaths remains unknown as it was never documented or recorded anywhere.

A year later, another pair of Siamese cats with kittens was imported to the United Kingdom by Eva Forestier Walker and her sister Ada, in 1886. These Siamese felines were less stocky in physique and sported longer more slender bodies. Their heads were not as rounded and it donned larger ears and wedge-shaped muzzles.

It is said that these distinct features and their differences from the Siamese cats they preceded was what drew strong impressions from their first-hand viewers. Hardly known or seen by Westerners during that period, were an early witness and viewer of the felines quoted to have described them as "an unnatural nightmare of a cat". Perhaps it was because of their odd coloration or their sharp blue eyes which merited this comment from the viewers - we can't say for sure. However, from then on, as the Siamese cat gained the curiosity and attention of cat-fanciers far and wide, it has shook off the initial comments and reaction of a select few.

British cat aficionados, over the next several years, imported a few more Siamese cats which collectively formed the initial breeding pool for the breed now known and loved in Great Britain. It is widely accepted that most Siamese cats living in Great Britain presently are direct descendants of the eleven original imports from Thailand, all of which arrived in the UK between the 1880's and the 1950's.

The Royal Cat Evolution

During their early days in the United Kingdom, the playful felines were given the moniker "Royal Cat of Siam". It is reflected on documentation that this breed was solely kept by and for Siamese royalty exclusively. However, later research did not turn up information or evidence of any organized breeding program within the royal courts of Siam.

Originally, the Siamese cats that were imported to the West were of medium size and sported varied physiques, and head shapes. Some sported long bodies that were muscular and notably agile and graceful with moderately wedge-shaped heads and ears were almost comically large yet in proportion to the measurement of their heads. Others carried slender bodies and sharper contoured heads. The cats were not extreme in size or form but its built ranged from a substantial size to a svelte physique.

As time passed the development of these felines were better controlled and the need for different classifications became a requirement to include felines that sported different color coats of varying length.

The last chapter of this book will give you information on regulations and requirements to show your Siamese buddy off at cat shows and cat walks. In the meantime, read on to find out more about what to expect when expecting a Siamese cat.

You've learnt that the Siamese cat is largely responsible for the other breeds of cats that have been developed over the years. The Himalayan cat, the Thai cat, the Ocicat, the Burmese, the Korat, the Snowshoe, the Tonkinese and a variety of Oriental breeds like the Oriental Longhair, the Oriental Shorthair, the Balinese, the Javanese as well as the Shorthair and Longhair Color -point all owe its beginnings to the beautiful Siamese cat.

The Siamese cat is indeed a special sort, having been instrumental and playing a big role in the emergence of these other equally attractive felines.

Informative Tidbits about the Siamese Cat

The Siamese of today bears very little resemblance to the first stock of the more moderate and traditional Siamese cats which sported visibly rounder heads and more rotund bodies. The old-school or traditional Siamese was eventually re-established by numerous breeders and registries and was later dubbed as the Thai cat.

According to the International Cat Association and countless Siamese guardians, the modern Siamese is an intelligent cat able to easily socialize with humans and other cat-friendly pets. It is described to be a playful sort and is known to be frolicsome from kitten hood way well into its adulthood.

Its tendency to seek and enjoy the company of other cats and humans is strong. Its frisky demeanor will certainly be infectious and you it will be hard to resist stopping to enjoy a pure moment of bliss with your Siamese feline.

The Siamese is a highly intelligent cat and is quite a talker who almost demands your attention when it has something to say and calls out to you. Exchanges in conversations with the Siamese cat will be amusing, engaging and cathartic. It is no wonder that the Siamese cat has gained greater popularity since its introduction to the Western world in the late 1880s.

The Siamese cat, in its modern day and old, traditional form is popular amongst the foundation stock of a number of other feline breeds. Through crossbreeding with other cats the Oriental Shorthair and the Color point Shorthair came about. This was executed to develop and expand the variety of coat patterns like the long-haired variety called the Himalayan. This procedure was likewise applied for hair-mutation breeds, namely, the Sphynx, the Peterbald and the Cornish Rex.

This graceful feline comes in two specifically distinct variations. The traditional one is with a slightly rotund body and an apple-shaped head and the more modern Siamese which sports a slender physique and has a large cranium. The latter is the sort who is popularly iconic and often thought of when the discussion of Siamese cats crop up.

The Traditional Siamese vs. the Modern Siamese

As the popularity of the Siamese cat increased between the 1950s to the 1960, breeders and judges of cat shows showed better favor to the more notably slender appearance of the Siamese feline. This turn of events instigated generations of selective breeding which produced the fine-boned, sleek bodied and narrow-headed felines.

The modern show Siamese cat was eventually bred to be visibly elongated, with a lean and tubular physique which stood on long, slender stems. Its graceful tail, very thin and very long, gradually tapers to a point. Its wedge-shaped head is graced with a pair of extremely big, wide-set ears which is one of the many stand out features of the Siamese cat.

Siamese cats of the more traditional or original form had largely disappeared from the cat show scene by the middle of the 1980s. However a few select breeders, in the UK particularly, went on to continue breeding and registering the traditional Siamese resulting in today's two kinds of Siamese cats.

The first kind is the standardized, modern day, show-style which is the Siamese we know today. The other sort is the Traditional Siamese. Both sorts come from and share similar distant ancestors but share few or no recent ancestors between them thereby forming effectively unique sub-breeds which have raised pressure to separate them entirely.

Today, in addition to the modern day Siamese breed category, The World Cat Federation (WCF) and The International Cat Association (TICA) accept Siamese cats that are of the less extreme sort along with the Wichiaanmat Cat which is directly imported from Thailand, under its present day breed name - the Thai cat.

Chapter Three: Siamese Cat Requirements

It is always important to consider the compatibility of guardian and pet when deciding to add a pet into the family dynamics. Many have made the mistake of adopting or buying a pet without prior research which had led to unnecessary heartache for the caregivers and pets suffering medical conditions that could have been avoided if only in depth research had been done initially.

Aside from health problems that may occur during the pet's lifetime, thinking long and hard about the transition flow is just as important. Preparation and getting ready for the actual integration is vital to ensuring a painless shift in the home dynamics not only for the pet but for everyone in the family involved.

In this chapter, you will find useful information about what it will take for you and your family to outfit your home and be new guardians to a Siamese cat.

Should You Opt for More Than One Siamese cat?

This is a question often asked by most potential pet owners. The reason for this frequent question being asked is because pet owners who have the best interests of the pet in mind want their pets to thrive not only physically but mentally as well.

The short answer is - yes! The Siamese cat and has always been noted to be very sociable and will certainly dote on the company of another elegantly dressed Siamese. In fact it will even welcome it. A good rule of thumb is when introducing a younger Siamese to an established Siamese, is to give both the new kitten and established cat ample time to get to know each other. Have them "investigate" each other from a safe distance and be watchful of their body language. Have another guardian present to avert and hinder any initial animosity or misgivings of the felines.

It is ideal to get two of them at the same time so that they grow up with each other. This is a painless method since introduction would have been done at the onset of the acquisition and they would likely be siblings from the same litter.

Many Siamese guardians have chosen to take in more than one Siamese cat to keep another in friendly company. They are highly trainable and if kept on a schedule they are better able to integrate themselves much easier with a family.

Cats and Humans

Felines have been some of the most misunderstood creatures of past and recent times. It was only of late when the University of Oregon studied the behavior of cats which they borrowed from homes and shelters to reveal evidence of their complex socio-cognitive and problem solving abilities.

These cats on loan were studied and observed to find out what really makes them "tick". The recent study has revealed a truth we would have otherwise shrugged off as fiction or even myth - that cats actually like your company more than anything else.

The felines in the program were deprived of food, toys and human interaction for a few hours. They were given stimulation related to the subjects of whom they were deprived of during the second stage of the experiment. What was revealed from the experiment, consisting of 50 cats from shelters and guardian homes, was astounding cats in fact dote and love the company of humans more than they enjoy food.

Not to say that if a feline were famished it would refuse food and would happily sit with you with a grumbling stomach, but this study proved that we have misunderstood felines to be unsociable, stuck up and selfish for a long time. The study showed that the truth is quite the opposite of the belief of mainstream culture.

Siamese cats are frolic, intelligent, sociable felines who practically live on the love and attention of its caregivers. Needing very little in terms of grooming, it does however enjoy staying in the company of its guardians and almost demands your undivided attention when you are at home with it. If you are the sort who tends to be away from home for extended periods, you may want to rethink taking in a Siamese cat as it can be susceptible to feline depression if left alone for too long.

If your heart is set on taking in a Siamese cat, consider taking in another Siamese cat to pair it with. As mentioned earlier, Siamese cats are sociable cats and are happiest when it is kept company by another Siamese cat, a cat-friendly canine or with a guardian who can be there for the feline during most times of the day.

Do Siamese Cats Get Along Well with Other Pets?

The Siamese cat is a docile, clever, agreeable and sweet-tempered feline. It has no problem sharing space and attention with other cats or cat-friendly dogs. You will soon discover that they are able to easily blend into families with more than one pet.

Of course, as with any family who chooses to integrate a new pet into their homes, your loving patience is vital to the success of introducing and welcoming a new Siamese into your home.

If this is your household, you will want to research not only the sociability of the Siamese cat you are introducing. You should also find out if your existing canine buddy will be friendly toward the cat. There are some dogs that do not get on well with cats and this is what you want to determine.

What does it Cost to take in a Siamese cat?

A new addition to the household always entails a shift in your monthly financial budget. Although Siamese cats require very minimal maintenance other than the occasional ear cleaning, brushing of teeth and coat as well as trimming of its nails, it will need initial and periodic inoculation as well as regular vet checkups.

In this section of this book, you will be able to determine if you are ready financially to acquire and be guardian to and care for a Siamese cat. You will be given an overview of what you could possibly be spending on your new Siamese cat/s. These would be inclusive of treat and toys, hygiene and grooming supplies, cat sundries, vet care, medical bills as well as sundries and their monthly food expenses.

Initial Costs

A Siamese cat from a reputable breeder on average would cost anywhere from $400-$600. Keep in mind that you would only want to deal with upstanding reputable breeders at this point as doing so will greatly ensure the future health of your Siamese cats.

Unscrupulous breeding practices have been the culprit of illnesses in Siamese cats and will result in a pile of medical bills and health issues that can be avoidable.

You will have to factor in inoculation of the cats, periodic visits to the vet to help ensure their overall good health, notarization later on as well as grooming tools, toys, equipment (like beds, dishes, scratching posts, litter boxes and kitty litter) and food.

Keeping your Siamese cat safely indoors reduces the risks of it coming into contact with feral cats, strays and large animals from which it may contract unwanted diseases or illnesses. It also secures your Siamese cat from violent attacks from much larger animals that may target your Siamese cat as prey.

Bringing in a Siamese cat to your home is quite the equal to rearing a child minus the yearly clothing bills and tuition. Consider these things as you sort out the kind of pet which will be best suited for your family and your finances.

What Are the Pros and Cons of Owning a Siamese cat?

Getting to know the sort and breed of pet you choose to acquire is a wise move. It is but sound to figure out if you and your household are ready to handle the responsibility of taking care of one or more Siamese cats.

Read on to gather more details regarding the pros and cons of taking in a Siamese cat.

Pros of Owning a Siamese Cat

This breed is…

- mild-tempered and amiable

- a gem at integrating itself well with its guardians

- highly trainable

- sociable and friendly to cat-friendly pets you already have

- generally quiet but can be quite a talker when stimulated, excited or in heat

Cons of Owning a Siamese Cat

This breed is...

- prone to asthma and aortic stenosis

- prone to feline depression if left on their own for extended periods

- can create quite a ruckus when in heat

Chapter Four: Acquiring Your Very Own Siamese Cats

You've come this far and have read up more on what it would take for you to adopt, take in or acquire a Siamese cat. It is now time for you to find out how to research procedures, seek out reputable breeders and to find out about humane methods of Siamese production which will ensure the future well-being and health of your Siamese cat.

This chapter aims to assist you in finding out who to talk to and where to acquire your very own Siamese cat.

Whether you choose to adopt or purchase one, here you will find information vital to the success and health of your would-be Siamese companion. You will also come across information that is aimed to help you cat-proof your home.

Where Should You Look to Acquire a Siamese Cat?

There are a number of avenues you can take in order to get a Siamese cat into your life. You may opt to visit your local pet store and inquire from them, but be wary and vigilant if this is the route you choose to take. Most pet stores will be able to furnish you with "papers proving breed authenticity" but it is not by any means a guarantee that the information on these papers is true and/or accurate.

Your best bet is to seek out reputable breeders who, like you, will be concerned about the future home the Siamese cat will be joining. Upstanding breeders will not only be open to answering your questions about their breeding methods and allowing you to see the Siamese cats in their living conditions, they will also be asking you a multitude of questions to figure out if the Siamese cat they will be releasing is going to a caring home.

You will also want to look into pet shelters and consider taking in a rescue cat before doling out wads of cash. Aside from saving a chunk of money, you'll also be doing a good deed of rescuing an animal that may otherwise have a bleak future ahead of it. You will surely find the rewards of rescuing a Siamese cat to be greatly rewarding. It will readily show its gratitude and love and stay your loyal companion for many years to come.

Things to Remember When Looking for a Reputable Breeder

Primarily, you will want to make certain that you only deal with an upstanding breeder as this will minimize the problems of taking in a sick kitten. Being in the know and ready for all eventualities is not only smart, it is an imperative.

The following are tips on seeking out an honest Siamese cat breeder:

- Collect and gather as much information as you possibly can about the breeders in your area. Get referrals from other Siamese cat guardians who are experienced and who may already have a database of reputable breeders. Network with and keep in contact with experienced Siamese guardians, groomers, pet shops and veterinary clinics - they can be good sources of information as to where you can find a healthy Siamese cat.

- Scrutinize and research breeders who have websites. Look up their reputation, ranking and license. Save yourself from frustration, stress and worry and only deal with breeders with a high success rate.

- Don't be taken for a ride. Ask questions and lots of them. Asking questions about breeding methods, procedures and practices ensures that you will be ready for any and all eventualities the Siamese may or may not encounter in the future.

- Ask about the breeder's program and what methods they employ during the mating period. Don't be afraid to ask for assurances - you need to be aware of what measures the breeder takes to largely eliminate or at the very least prevent the transmission of congenital conditions that can be passed on to young Siamese kittens.

- Immediately turn away from breeders on your list who give flowery, shady, dodgy and seemingly uninformed responses. Make certain that you deal only with breeders who have a good success rate and have been reputed to be humane in dealing with the breeding process.

- Do not think twice about eliminating breeders on your list who refuse to answer questions you may ask about the cats' history, health, method of breeding and anything else related to the future welfare and overall well-being of the feline.

- Hop into your car and take a road trip. Ask to visit the breeder's facilities. A breeder who has nothing to hide will welcome you immediately and will gladly give you a tour around their facilities. You want to look at the facilities with your own eyes and check out if the shelter is kept sanitary. Willingness and transparency to attend to and respond to queries from possible Siamese caregivers is a positive attribute and these breeders should be marked for strong consideration.

- Upstanding breeders will also be asking their own set of questions. These breeders are not just out to make a quick buck. They are equally concerned about the future wellbeing of the feline and will ask questions that will determine if you are indeed a suitable caregiver of this precious life.

- If you decide on purchasing a Siamese kitten, you will have to place a deposit to get the ball rolling. Do not forget to ask about the breeders terms as finances will be discussed. Once you and the breeder come to an agreement, you can mark off one of the first tasks on your list as done. Make sure that you are furnished with papers that would reflect your initial payment and that all sundries are itemized.

Adopt a Siamese cat from a Rescue

Adopting from a shelter is one sure fire way of dissuading the operations of shady, fly-by-night breeders. It also garners you points for a good deed done when you opt to rescue a Siamese from a bleak future.

This avenue to acquiring a Siamese entails very little in terms of initial investment and the returns are far greater than you would ever imagine. The insurmountable benefits of adopting a Siamese cat is limitless and if you are lucky enough you might just find one ready and waiting for your loving care at a nearby shelter.

The obvious and distinct difference of getting a Siamese cat from a reputable breeder to rescuing one from an uncertain future at a pet shelter is with the latter you would have given the poor feline a chance at living a better life and being in a home that it deserves.

A rescue Siamese may also have the advantage of being house trained and housebroken which allows you more quality time into getting to know the cat as well as getting it integrated with yourself and your family. Keep in mind that the Siamese cat with its friendly, jovial and frisky personality makes integration and introduction to the family and easier job and will seem less of a task. Being that it is one of the more mild-mannered of the feline specie, getting them blended into your daily routine will almost be like taking a walk in the park.

List of Websites of Breeders and Rescue Adoption

<u>Siamese Cat Breeders</u>

TICA
<http://www.tica.org/find-a-breeder/item/324-siamese-breeders>

Life With Siamese Cats

<http://www.life-with-siamese-cats.com/siamese-cat-breeders.html>

Cat Breed

<http://www.catbreedslist.com/>

<u>**Rescue Adoption**</u>

Petfinder

<https://www.petfinder.com/cat-breeds/siamese>

Siamese Rescue

<https://www.siameserescue.org/>

Adopt a Pet

<http://www.adoptapet.com/s/siamese-cats-for-adoption>

Love to Know

<http://cats.lovetoknow.com/Siamese_Kittens_for_Adoptio n>

Life with Siamese Cats Rescue

<http://www.life-with-siamese-cats.com/siamese-rescue.html>

Another Bit of Siamese cat Trivia

Although the record of the longest living cat is held by another feline of a different sort who presently lives in Texas, the longest living Siamese cat to date is reported to be living a happy and content existence at the age of 30 years old. A 30-year-old Siamese cat! It's almost impossible to wrap your head around that fact.

Recognized and lauded by the Guinness Book of World Records, Scooter, was born many years ago on March 26 during the Reagan administration.

Scooters' guardian, Gail Floyd, cites Scooters' love for travel has kept him active and healthy all these years. Having had visited 45 states, he is possibly one of the most well-travelled felines of his time.

Although Scooter is a very special exception, Siamese cats have been recorded to live healthy lives for as long as 15 years. Its normal lifespan is anywhere from 11-15 years given the proper care and medical attention it may need.

Selecting a Healthy Siamese cat

Siamese cats are not as susceptible to diseases as most other cats are. Your choices at the stage of selection of breeders and the task of learning more about the feline and the family tree and history of the cat which you choose to adopt or acquire is of great importance. Of course, you will want to talk to your vet about its health and what it is prone to so as to avoid exposing them to these health conditions.

The maintenance and upkeep of a Siamese cat is quite minimal. Apart from periodical medical checkups and its nutritional needs, it can be considered a low maintenance cat who requires very little in terms of the occasional grooming which you can carry out on your own.

At the onset of grooming practices it would be wise to employ the aide of another caregiver. Later on as the feline gets used to its routine, it will be much easier to carry out these necessary tasks.

At this stage, making certain that you have covered all the bases to ensure a happy, healthy new addition to your home is of vital importance.

- **Behavior Around Humans:** Generally known to be mild-tempered and sociable, if a Siamese cat is aloof around humans or is skittish then it may have possibly gone through some sort of abuse and/or neglect from the previous humans with which it cohabitated. Felines, much like most pets will recall trauma, especially if you choose to adopt one from a pet shelter. In this case, you will need to have greater patience. Traumatized pets will need a little more time to get used to its' new and loving surroundings.

- **Mobility:** Have a look and make sure that the feline is able to walk well and is mobile on its own without hindrance or difficulty. Bless your heart if you choose to adopt one with an existing injury. Should you have a big heart and be open to adoption then you have to also be aware that you will be largely responsible for medical bills and possibly more frequent visits to the vet.

- **Tail:** All felines tend to develop arthritis on their tails as they age and mature. Remember to be gentle when handling the tail of any feline to avoid injury. With feathered strokes, gently run the ball of your palm up and down the Siamese tail. Never, at any cost, handle a cat by its tail.

- **Cat-friendly Pet Interaction:** Your presence will be of great importance at the stage of introduction of your Siamese to existing pets you may own and when welcoming it to its new home and refuge. Keep in mind that there are some pets that can be hostile toward others. Don't make the mistake of just bringing home an additional furry buddy without research and preparation. You can avoid this stressful situation by doing in-depth research if your established pet is a cat-friendly one.

- **Appetite:** Siamese cats have moderate appetites. Over - feeding any pet is strongly discouraged to avoid health issues that may hamper the pets' good health. Most cats are and can be susceptible to feline arthritis. Overfeeding and unscheduled offerings of food and treats could lead to obesity which could later be cause for the cat suffers from arthritis. A heavy set cat will have greater difficulty carrying its weight. This will limit its natural movements of jumping and skittering around.

- **Body Appearance:** Scrutinize and examine the fur, body, ears, and legs of the cat. Check for nicks, bald spots, lumps or hardness under its skin. Keep in mind to be very gentle with its tail and limbs, never handle a feline by its legs or its tail. Rough and extreme handling of its tail and limbs will most certainly cause it pain, discomfort and can be cause of preventable medical issues.

- **Coat:** Gently run your bare fingers through its coat as you look for signs of fleas or ticks that the cat may exhibit. It will be easy to spot if the Siamese suffers from this as it has fur that is close to its skin. Be vigilant and watch your feline for excessive scratching and skin gnawing. To minimize the occurrence of fleas and ticks, keep your Siamese indoors. Limit its outside excursions to a regular minimum and give it a bath once a month with pet-approved shampoo. Give it a regular brush after playtime, when it has spent its energy, and is in a relaxed state.

- **Eyes:** The eyes should be discharge free, almond-shaped and bright. The color of the eyes is to be a stark, vivid, tanzanite-blue. Due to the tyrosine mutation resulting in abnormality in the neurological connections between its eyes and brain some Siamese cats have the appearance of being cross-eyed; this is nature's way of compensating for the trait and allows the cat to see well. Because of selective breeding this trait is seen far less in Siamese cats today. However if you do choose one that may later display this trait be aware that the cat will have more challenges focusing and seeing in the dark. Again, keeping your Siamese indoors is strongly recommended.

- **Ears:** Ears are to be clean and wax free. Look out for tiny nicks that may be an invitation for infections. It is imperative that the Siamese cat's ears be kept pristine. Cleaning its ears requires very little; a soft cloth moist with lukewarm water will do the job. Do not make the mistake of introducing cotton buds to clean its ears as this may cause injury to its eardrums. This, even in humans, can be dangerous and cause more harm than good.

- **Mouth and Teeth:** Look out for any deformities or abnormalities like protruding teeth. The upper and lower lip of the Siamese is to be aligned with each other. Breathing is not to be made out of the mouth. Its upper and lower lips should be aligned to each other. If you plan on showing your Siamese later on at shows, these details will be things that judges will be studying to determine if it meets their association's pedigree regulations.

- **Belly or Stomach:** Scrutinize the feline for signs of a swollen belly or lumps around the stomach area. Look out for bald spots that may indicate fungal infections that may spread to other parts of the body.

- **Anal Area:** With gentle care, lift its tail to check the Siamese cat's anal area to ensure that it is clean. As with cleaning its ears, use a soft cloth moistened with warm water.

Important Note

Reputable breeders will only release a Siamese kitten when it is 12 weeks old. It is highly advised though that separation from the mother is best put off until the kitten has weaned off the teat. Delay bringing home the kitten until it is ready to eat solid foods.

How to Feline-Proof Your Home

Siamese cats are jovial, friendly cats with a very pleasing temperament. And although they are pretty well-rounded felines, it is still quite important to note how to keep your new ward safe as its new caregiver. The following information aims to help you to start preparing and fitting your home to welcome your new furry friend.

- Keep food out of sight and reach. Store them in cupboards or stack them in a closed pantry away from your buddy. Make sure that any food that is set outside the fridge or pantry is sealed in tightly covered spill-proof containers. Clapping and calling out the name of your Siamese usually does the job of dissuading it from further mischief and curiosity.

- Felines have a natural tendency to hunt, rummage and scrounge for food and curiosities. Stave off this innate habit of theirs by making certain your trash bins are tightly covered and won't spill out in the event of cat curiosity.

- Cats are naturally curious and will usually play with small objects that they can push around and play with. Store away tiny valuables if you suspect your little fur ball is the sort of cat who likes to play with small, shiny objects. You will have to make sure that there are no loose strings or hanging ropes they could get tangled in, so keeping wires folded or protected from unwanted gnawing is a measure you would want to take to somehow guarantee its safety.

- Vitamins, medication, and/or prescription drugs are to be kept away from its reach and hidden from sight. The dangers of having your feline ingest a meant-for-human pill is the last thing you want to happen and will warrant a trip to the emergency room. The discomfort the cat has to endure to expel this from its body can be uncomfortable. Best that caregivers avoid this preventable trip to vet by keeping all medicine locked away.

- Cleaning supplies you use around the home usually contain highly toxic chemicals which can poison and cause great harm your new friend. Do store them away where your Siamese kitten can't see or find these products which will certainly cause them great harm.

- Should your feline be allowed to wander around the house and its perimeter make certain that you do not neglect to cat-proof your garage too. Cats are known to prefer perching on high places. Make sure that there is no heavy equipment or tools which they may push over the edge which may hurt them or people in the home.

- This bit is very important for those who have house plants or foliage growing around their home; there are many, countless plants that pose danger to felines. Determine that the greenery surrounding your home is non - toxic to your Siamese cat. In the event that you determine that there are plants in or around your homes which are toxic to your feline, consider replanting them away from the area where your cat is allowed to roam. You may also opt to barricade these plants or altogether replace them with plants that are non - toxic to cats. Poisoning from plants which are toxic or harmful when ingested by cats is a very real concern and should be high on your list of things to avoid.

- Keep in mind that cats have a tendency to get carried away when they are at play. Dealing with more than one pet can also be quite a handful. To avoid the possibility of electrocution when your feline is in a curious mood or when rough housing with their furry pals, use plastic covers to plug unused electrical sockets.

- It is not a surprise that some cats have an aversion to gnawing at strings, ropes and electric wires that mimic string. Feline-proof exposed wires with those nifty wire covers that will discourage them from chewing on a live wire which their teeth may damage and cause them electrocution.

There are a lot more tips than what is listed here to keep your Siamese cat safe within your home. These preventive and safety tips will not only benefit your friendly feline, it will also serve you and your family well so that you can keep your home intact and safe from accidents. Remove things that can be harmful to your feline and any minimize the possible incidence of danger posed to your family members.

Chapter Five: Living with Your Siamese Cats

Realize that taking on any pet, whether it be a canine or feline entails great responsibility that isn't be taken lightly. Many pet guardians and caregivers have likened taking in pets to raising children. Of course not all aspects of rearing pets and children share similarities but in terms of taking charge and identifying situations which may pose danger to either have been cited as similar.

Doing the initial research to ensure that you and other possible caregivers need to be aware of is stressed with great importance. Your willingness to take on the responsibilities of being guardian to one will be the foundation of its well - being in the years to come. The idea of taking in a pet may seem romantic and easy but don't be deceived by misleading beliefs. Pets do greatly depend on the discipline and responsibility of its humans to lead a successful and healthy life.

Arm and empower yourself with vital knowledge and crucial information on how to provide a good, happy and healthy home life to your new chatty buddy, the Siamese cat. Learn more about how you can set up spaces and areas for your cat, Outfit spaces in your home that will provide the Siamese its basic, everyday needs such as a toilet area, its play space, and a dining spot. You will also want to create safe boundaries that flank your house where your cat is given freedom to wander under your watchful supervision.

Habitat and Activity Needs for Siamese Cats

No matter the number of similarities a particular breed shares, it is wise to keep in mind that each individual feline is different from each other. However it is safe to surmise that all cats will thrive best in homes where they feel wanted, protected, loved, cared for and where they feel safe. The chatterbox Siamese is no different this way from other pets.

Now just because the Siamese is generally mild-tempered and easy to deal with it is not to say that it could get itself into mischief given the right conditions. Stimulating the feline with frequent, regular playtime and exercise is a must in order to channel their feisty energy and will safely engage them.

This a good time to remind you once again that a Siamese cat is best kept as an indoor cat. Their unique exotic, physical qualities make them quite an eye catcher and you will want to avoid getting your cat taken by individuals who may fancy their friendly disposition and one-of-a-kind look. Forays outside of the home should be supervised and be kept to a minimum. These measures will ensure the safety of the feline from large animal attacks and the possibility of contracting diseases that can be passed on from an ill animal.

There are many varieties of plants that pose danger to felines. Make the wise choice of knowing what plants flank your home and make arrangements to replant, fence off or replace the foliage surrounding your home to add a measure of security that will keep your cat healthy and safe.

Keeping Your Siamese cat Healthy and Fit

Channel your Siamese cat's seemingly boundless energy by employing and utilizing toys that will engage and stimulate them. The clever Siamese is a highly trainable feline that can be taught to fetch and retrieve objects which they can carry, much to the delight and fascination of many Siamese guardians.

Use toy lasers, feather teasers, plush toys and bouncy balls that will encourage them to blow off energy in a positive manner that is not destructive to itself, other people in the family and furniture inside the home. Always handle your cat with care as felines are known to develop arthritis more than other pets.

Toward of giving your home and furniture the clawed-and-scratched look, you will have to outfit and make room for a scratching post or two in your home.

Equipment You Need to Supply for Your Siamese cat

Siamese cats like most felines are some of the easiest pets to potty train. That being said, you will still be tasked to delegating areas where your Siamese can do its "business" when "nature calls". The wise ratio of cat to litter box is 1:2. Two litter boxes per cat ensure that your cat will not become constipated. A cat hates nothing more than doing its business in a soiled box. More so a soiled box used by another feline! Avoid this by cleaning out the cat's litter box regularly and when needed.

Keep the litter boxes in social areas of the home where they can do their business in peace. You may opt to keep them slightly concealed from prying eyes by tucking them underneath cat-approved plants or nooks around the house

There are countless choices of cat litter which are scented that will help keep hygiene in check. Make certain that the litter boxes are kept clean at all times. Ideally, clean out a litter box as soon as it is soiled. At the very least, make sure that you routinely check on its cleanliness twice a day. This will ensure that the feline will have no qualms of doing their business when nature pays a visit.

For holidays and extended vacations with the family, a sturdy and durable cat-carrier is recommended for out-of-town forays, road trips and short excursions around your locality. It will also double up well as a cat bed for extended periods away from home. Be sure to line it with a familiar blanket that has the scent of home to lessen the impact of being in new and unfamiliar surroundings.

A useful piece of equipment to employ during downtime is a good, sturdy brush that you can use as a tool for bonding. Brushing your feline not only creates strength in your bond with your feline, it will also help the proper circulation of skin oils essential to keep its skin in pristine condition.

Choose for it a nice warm and comfortable bed for it curl into, warm up in and a place to laze about. If you have a sun porch set out a soft mat where it can soak in some rays and enjoy a nice breeze as you enjoy the day with it.

A nice warm bed that it can crawl into when it's all tuckered out from a day of play and socialization will be one of the more important sundries you will need to provide for your feline. A familiar blanket that can double up as a "jungle gym" and nap area will be ideal as well.

Rethink plastic feeding dishes and opt for ceramic or stainless bowls for their food and water. It may take a few tries before you find foods which your new pet prefers.

Think twice about choosing plastic feeding and drinking bowls. Instead opt for the more sanitary and much more durable stainless feeding bowls that are sans toxic chemicals that may be harmful to your Siamese feline.

Siamese cats are much more prone to mouth infections and gum disease. Be sure to ask your vet how to brush your Siamese cat's teeth properly. You may ask to observe the first few times your vet or cat groomer does it and follow the same steps when you are at home.

Investing on the sturdier sort of equipment and grooming sundries is very important, lest you plan on spending more frequently for supplies that do not last. Do not scrimp on the tools that you and your feline will be using frequently as it matures.

The Personality of a Siamese Cat

The Siamese cat is an expressively vocal feline who can be quite opinionated and talkative. They are the sort who will not hold back on telling you exactly what is on their minds. Siamese cats are experts in gaining your attention using their loud, raspy voice as their tool to get your attention. Siamese cats require you to pay them mind when talked to and for you to act according to their advice.

This breed of cats has a strong tendency to attach themselves to their human caregivers, often building a strong bond with one person particularly. The Siamese is extremely "helpful" and may think itself to be your assistant - shadowing your every move around the household and supervising your movements and activities around the house.

It is a sort that will enjoy downtime sitting on your lap whilst you relax and lounge. The Siamese is the sort that would climb into bed with you and get under the sheets and stake its claim on a space of your shared pillow.

If you are the sort who does not enjoy back-talk or chatter, the Siamese cat may not be the companion you seek. On the flip side, if you find pleasure in chatter, conversation and company as the day progresses, the Siamese cat will instantly win a place in your heart and will soon be your best friend. Make certain that you factor in essential quality time with it as the Siamese is known not only to be a very sociable feline but a demanding one too.

The Siamese cat will not be pleased if it is left on its own for extended periods of time. So if you are set on acquiring a Siamese cat, make sure that there is someone left at home during your absence to keep it company. Many Siamese cat guardians smartly opt to take in two Siamese cats so that the cats can keep each other company during periods of the day when the caregiver is away.

This feline from the shores of Thailand is known to be highly intelligent. It is athletic, very agile, and playfully frisky. Keep your Siamese cat's brain active, engaged and busy by utilizing puzzle toys during playtime.

Be part of and assist in its daily physical exercise regimen by employing teaser toys that the feline can chase around the house. Provide it a big cat tree which it can clamber onto and jump off of, for an all-around, good workout.

The Siamese is a naturally curious feline who will venture into the house looking for adventure or mischief if you do not pay mind to leaving him some kind of constructive distraction (like the leaving TV switched on, leaving a mechanical toy that it can play with) whilst you are out. Failure to do so may result in rolls of toilet paper unrolled and scattered around your home.

Make playtime a time for you and your Siamese cat to bond and catch up. Remember that the Siamese cat thrives on the attention and company of its guardians and will want nothing more than to spend some much needed one-on-one interaction with you.

If you are in strong consideration of a Siamese cat, you will need to factor in making time for the cat in your daily schedule. If you are the kind of person who is required to fly out of town at a moment's notice, you may want to rethink getting a Siamese cat, unless you are prepared and willing to spend a considerable amount of money paying pet hotels and pet sitters.

Temperament

Renowned for their utterly sociable nature and demeanor, Siamese cats are highly intelligent and openly affectionate to caregivers and other pets alike. They are described and characterized as extroverts who immensely enjoy being surrounded by the company of people.

They are known to build strong bonds with one person and its loyalty is apparent through this union. The Siamese cat is an extremely vocal feline with a loud, low-pitched tone known as the "Meezer" - a word from which one of its nicknames is from derived. Its voice has been likened to the crying of a human baby and demands attention with persistence.

The Siamese cat is naturally playful and quite active even into adulthood. They are often chronicled to display behavior resembling that of a dog more than it is likened to other felines.

If left alone for an extended period of time, Siamese cats may be prone to cat-blues and bouts of feline depression. This is why Siamese cats are often bought in twos - the benefits are not only to police the other but it is also one way to stave off boredom and to keep each other company whilst their caregiver is away.

Chapter Six: Nutritional Needs of Siamese Cats

This section of the book is aimed at discussing the nutrition and food your Siamese cat will require. It will reveal what you should and should not feed your feline to successfully raise it. You will find out about foods that it requires for a healthy life and foods which are bad for them and that you should thereby avoid.

Like all things living, a feline's health hinges on the quality of food it eats. Make it your business to understand what your cat needs in order to stave off sickness. Your diligence in this matter of feeding and food will pay off in the long run and you will think yourself for thinking ahead.

The Nutritional Needs of Siamese Cats

Siamese cats are carnivores. Unlike other felines the Siamese is able to tolerate table food in moderate portions. It is still advisable that the caregiver prepare cat meals without the usual seasonings one would normally put in dishes for human consumption.

This is a good time to remind you that the Siamese cat shares ancestry with some of the bigger wild cats we know of today. Wild cats are far from being vegetarians and so is your Siamese cat.

To avert frustration, like your Siamese cat falling ill or having to spend insane amounts of cash buying large bags of food it won't touch, you'll need to know what it needs and introduce these to the feline once it is ready to eat solid foods. Knowing is the first step to successful and nutritional feeding. Their adorably cute faces, tummies and general health hinge on your thoughtful diligence on what foods you feed it.

Raw Feeding or Commercial Food

All cats are carnivores and once upon a time, in its wild habitat, it would hunt for prey to eat. The advent of humans caring for and domesticating felines has introduced cats to foods it would normally not eat in the wild. It also opened up the door to commercially available food. These commercially produced foods contain calories and ingredients which your cat does not need nor require. In fact many of these foods in the market may lead to health issues because of the additives put into branded foods.

Should you opt to feed your Siamese commercially made cat food, you will need to be very selective and finicky about what brand you bring home. You should read the labels printed on the products - make sure that you do proper research so as to understand what ingredients make up the food.

It is probably not unknown to many (but is wise to reminded) that pet-food manufacturers take advantage of the fact that many cat guardians blindly take the advice of marketing advertisements to be true. Do not fall in this category.

Knowing what ingredients make up store-bought pet food is the first step to avoiding all sorts of maladies that an undernourished cat can suffer.

Raw feeding is a convenient and fuss-free manner of feeding your feline. It eliminates the fuss of hits-and-misses of commercially store-bought foods and you can ensure quality control over the food being eaten by your pet because you will be picking the cuts and portions. You will also have a level of control because you will be able to guarantee freshness of the meats.

Protein

Be sure that your Siamese cat's meals include meats and lots of it in reasonable portions. You can opt to slowly introduce raw foods to them or you may transition by boiling and chopping up a variety of meat to serve it during meals. You may choose to give it chicken, veal, beef and occasionally some liver. You may also ask your vet or a seasoned Siamese guardian for tips and suggestions. However, do remember that in the end the responsibility of feeding your feline falls on your shoulders. So read up on the best ways to successfully raise your cat and the sort of food it requires staying healthy.

Fat

There are certain fats that your cat requires in order to transmit and distribute nutrients from the food it eats. Fat is a concentrated source of energy and is partly responsible in metabolic regulation and cell integrity. Omega 3 and Omega 6 fatty acids are present in animal meats and is important to the health of a feline.

Minerals

Minerals play a big role in almost all physiological reactions. Minerals play the role of enzyme formation, nutrient utilization, transporting oxygen, PH balance. Mineral intake is stored in the muscle tissue and bones.

Water

Always keep your feline well hydrated and make sure that it has access to clean drinking water at any given time. Hydration is very important most especially if you choose to feed it dry foods bought from the store. Dry foods do not contain the moisture as in raw foods so augmenting its liquid intake with fresh water is a must.

Feeding Transition

If you are considering transitioning your cat from dry foods to raw feeding, be aware that it will probably take time for your cat to get used to this. If your cat has been used to certain store-bought foods and you want to feed it more naturally, you will have to slowly introduce raw food to the cat in small portions gradually increasing servings as it learns to appreciate raw food.

Do not make the mistake of making your cat go cold-turkey; that is almost equal to starving the poor feline. Instead slowly replace portions of its regular food with raw foods until it gets used to the texture and taste of it. You will find that cats being carnivores will not take long to developing a liking for it.

Chapter Seven: Showing Your Siamese Cat

Many cat aficionados find great joy in showing off their Siamese buddy for people to admire and get to know.

This last chapter of this book is geared toward giving you, the reader, and information on the CFA Breeding Standards. Find out if your Siamese is eligible for registry with the Cat Fanciers Association and learn what requirements are sought out during the showing and judging of a Siamese at cat show events.

Whether show quality or otherwise, your Siamese cat will display outright affection and fondness to your longing kindness and repay you with undying loyalty and gratitude. You will surely enjoy the company and companionship of this clever and sometimes outspoken feline for many years to come now that you have come to understand what is needed from you as its guardian and lifelong friend.

<u>Appearance</u>

Today's breed standard of the modern day Siamese cat requires that the cat sport a tubular, elongated and muscular physique. Its head is to be in perfect triangular form from the tip of each of its ears to the top of its nose.

Its expressive eyes are a stark color of blue and it is hypnotizing almond-shaped, while its ears, large and wide-based on its cranium are positioned slightly more toward the sides of its head.

The Siamese cat breed has a long, graceful neck and a long tapered tail. Its pale coat is short, fine, glossy and sticks to the body sans undercoat. Its unique pointed color pattern and light blue eyes sets it apart from its close relation, the Oriental Shorthair.

Today's amiably lovable, present day Siamese cat shares its pointed color scheme with the original or more traditional Thai cat. However, the differences in both its head shape and body type are unique features that distinguish one cat from the other.

The curiously pointed color pattern of the very vocal Siamese cat is due to a form of partial albinism which came about from a mutation of the enzyme partially responsible in the production of melanin. The mutated enzyme is heat-sensitive and fails to function at normal body temperatures.

It, however, is more active in the cooler areas of the feline's skin thereby resulting in the darker coloration on the coolest body parts of the feline. These cooler parts include its extremities and its face which is cooled down by the passing of air through the feline's sinuses.

All Siamese kittens are born white or pure cream and begin to display visible points on colder parts of its body during the first few months of its life. When the Siamese kitten reaches its four week mark, the points should ideally show and clearly stand out becoming more noticeable with the pronounced and apparent coloration.

As the Siamese cat matures its skin coloration tends to darken more with age. An adult Siamese who lives in a warm climate, sports a lighter colored coat unlike its counterparts which reside in places with cooler climate. The majority of Siamese cats originally had seal points in extremely dark brown color which almost looks black.

Occasionally though Siamese cats are produced with blue points, which appear more like a cool gray, and is the result of a genetic dilution of seal point. The lighter brown or chocolate points is a genetic variation of seal point and the lilac point, appearing as a pale, warm gray is a genetic dilution of the chocolate points.

At first, these colors were thought to be inferior seal points and were disqualified for breeding or showing. These shades were all eventually embraced and welcomed by breeder associations and have become more prevalent with the aide of breeding programs specifically geared toward producing the variety of hues.

Outcrossing Siamese cats with other breeds later developed Siamese-mix felines sporting points of new patterns and colors which include Red and Cream point, the tabby or lynx point as well as the torte or the tortoiseshell point.

All pointed Siamese-style cats are classified part of the Siamese breed in Great Britain. The Cat Fanciers Association, a major cat registry in the United States, merely considers the four original colors of the Siamese feline which are the seal point, lilac point, chocolate point and blue point in its registry. Felines of the Oriental Shorthair sort with color points in patterns or hues not of the classified four colors are tagged and classified as color point Short hairs in the registry. This classification was adopted by the World Cat Federation and treats the Short hair with colour points as totally distinct breed from the Siamese cat.

Many of the Siamese cats which came from Thailand once had a kink in their tails and the noticeable trait was thought and considered to be a flaw. Breeders, over time, have been able to successfully eradicate this tail imperfection in the Siamese cat's tail. However the kinked tail phenomena are still widely present amongst many street cats roaming the alleys and byways of Thailand.

Coat Color and General Appearance

The original pointed pattern of the Siamese was the outcome of a genetic mutation and the feline itself is of a breed which is natural. The Siamese cat played a large role in the creation and development of many various cat breeds amongst which include the Himalayan division of the Persian cat, the Tonkinese cat, the Havana Brown cat, The Oriental cat and the Balinese cat to name a few.

The appearance of the Siamese cat hinges on the breed standard set by each individual cat organization. Most feline associations require the Siamese feline to sport a muscular but svelte physique with long lines. Its head, wedge-shaped, long and tapering is to form a triangle from the narrow tip of the nose outward to the top of its large ears.

The unusually big ears of the Siamese are wide at the base of the head and the tips of the ears are to be pointed on its ends, giving it an overall triangular appearance. A deep, hypnotizing hue of deep blue is the color of the Siamese signature almond-shaped eyes.

Its body, which is often described as tubular, rests on long, slender stems - its hind legs a tad higher than the fore legs. The Siamese cat pads are round on tiny, delicate, oval-shaped paws and its long, thin tail tapers to a fine point of elegance.

The coat of the Siamese is short and has a texture that is fine and smooth. The breed standards of the Cat Fanciers Association (CFA) states that Siamese cats have four distinct shades of color; chocolate point, an ivory body sporting milk chocolate-colored points and cinnamon-pink nose leather and paw pads; seal point, a pale fawn to cream body with deep seal brown points and deep brown nose leather and paw pads; blue point, a bluish-white body with deep blue points and slate-colored nose leather and paw pads; and lilac point, a pristinely glacial-white body with frosty pinkish-gray points and lavender-pink nose leather and paw pads.

The International Cat Association permits a range of shades, hues and patterns outside and beyond the four point colors that are recognized and accepted by the Cat Fanciers Association. These include red points, cream points, smoke points, tabby points and silver points.

CFA Breeding Standards

Breed Council regulations state that a Siamese cat which is purebred is eligible for registration with CFA is to show proof of an 8-generation pedigree which consists ONLY of Siamese previously registered. This is to say that on an 8-generation pedigree, each of the cats registered, have purebred Siamese as its direct ancestors.

There are other cat registry organizations that still register cats which display color - point shorthairs (tabby/lynx points, red/cream points, or tortie-points) or Oriental Shorthairs on its pedigree as Siamese. This is when a cat is registered according to how it appears and not based on the cat's pedigree. This is also known as a phonotypical registry.

CFA is a pedigree-based registry for felines and in addition to requiring a show of proof of 8-generation pure pedigree also requires a Siamese to display the four classic colors of seal point, blue point, chocolate point, or lilac point.

For many decades the CFA has only accepted registries of Siamese which sport the four colors mentioned above. The reasoning for this rule is that these colors are considered to be the colors naturally occurring in Siamese cats that are pure bred.

Other patterns such as tortie, lynx or solids like cinnamon and red suggest hybridization therefore unacceptable and goes against the Associations rules of registering only purebred Siamese cats. Felines with these colors and patterns are hybrid breeds produced using the Siamese during the initial breeding process.

Here are the criteria considered by the CFA when judging Siamese at shows.

Overall Condition

The term condition mirrors the wellness and totality of the feline. Environment, diet, care and heredity are all vitally important roles in the production of a well-conditioned feline. Each facet of the cat is to reflect the outcome of these factors which are important during judging.

The show feline must be in prime physical condition. It should be faultlessly clean. Emphasizing the beauty of the breed, grooming should enhance the feline's beauty.

Its temperament is to be well-balanced and the show cat has to be receptive during the procedure of judging. It should display a calm and stable disposition which will enhance the feline and allow the judge to display the feline and evaluate it to the feline's best advantages.

The Siamese well-bring, its vigor and general health are to be reflected through clear eyes, a shiny coat of fur and it is to be alert. During movement, the cat is to exhibit the beauty and grace natural to its breed.

During the showing of the feline, a judge will record the shape and size of its bones structure, its muscle tone as well as the basic conformation of the feline. The SUM of its parts is made up of the TOTAL CAT.

In order to embody the aesthetic qualities of grace, beauty and agility which epitomize the feline, the ideal show feline must reflect sound structure and excellent health. Pedigreed cat breed variations in structure help in distinguishing and differentiating it. Individual breed standards may sometimes describe unusual physical traits, but the ideal show cat should be free of any exaggerated characteristics or otherwise, which may cause discomfort to the feline or jeopardize its health and well-being.

The mature cranium is to be smooth visibly and to the touch sans any undesirable protuberances or depressions. The eyes are to be bright and clear with movements that synced are coordinated. It must not be cross-eyed. The feline's breathing is to be effortless. The mouth of the cat should close with proper occlusion. Its jaw and face are to be aligned and symmetrical to each other.

The skeletal frame should function in balance and symmetry. The vertebrae are aligned without deviation or fixation. The joints are flexible and the spine supple. The legs fully support movement and weight and are parallel.

The body shape is to be smoothly contoured from the gentle outward curve of the chest to the softer continuous line of the stomach and abdomen. The feline's muscular development of the shoulders, its midsection to the feline's hind quarters is to reflect strength and compatibility with its body shape and style.

What should never be forgotten and is to be kept in thoughtful consideration is that the feline is a breathing, living, mobile being. Its function and sound structure is integral in the search of the overall aesthetic of the cat.

General

The ideal Siamese, according to CFA breed standards, is to be of medium size, svelte and slender; a refined feline sporting long line that taper. It is muscular but very lithe. Males are often larger proportionally. Refinement and balance is the core of the breed, that when all parts are considered they all blend in harmony as a whole, not giving too little or too much consideration to one singular feature.

Head

It is to sport a long tapering wedge. The head is to be of medium size and is in proper proportion to its body. The whole wedge begins at the nose and spreads out in straight lines to the top of its ears forming a triangle, leaving no breaks at the whiskers. The space width between the eyes should be no more than the size of an eye. The underlying bone structure must be apparent when the whiskers are smoothed back. Allowance must be given for the jowls of a stud feline.

Skull

It must sport a flat skull. When viewed in profile, a straight long line is to be visible from the tip of the head to the end of its nose. There is to be no bulge over its eyes and there is to be no dip in the nose.

Ears

Ears are to be strikingly but proportionally large, must be sticking up and pointed on its head, wide at the base trailing the lines of the wedge.

Eyes

Eyes must be almond-shaped and of medium size. Eyes should neither be recessed nor should it protrude.

Eyes are to slant toward the nose showing harmony with wedge lines and ears. Eyes should not be crossed.

Nose

Nose should display continuation with the lines of the wedge and should be long and straight.

Muzzle

Muzzle is to be wedge-shaped and fine.

Chin and Jaw

It must be medium in size. Both chin and nose should be lined up on a similar vertical plane. Neither should recede nor be massively excessive.

Body

The body of the Siamese is to be of medium built, displayed gracefully as long and svelte. It is to show a distinct combination of firm muscles and fine bones. Shoulders and hips must be in harmony and display continuity running the same sleek lines of a tubular body. Its hips should not be wider than its shoulders and its abdomen should be tight.

Neck

Its neck is to be long and slender

Legs

The legs of the Siamese are to be slim and long. Its hind legs are to be higher than its fore - quarters and must be in proper proportion to its body.

Paws

Its paws should be small, dainty and oval. Its toes should have five in front and four.at the rear.

Tail

Its tail is to be thin, long, and must taper to a fine point.

Coat

The coat of the Siamese must be fine textured, short and glossy. The feline's coat must lies close to the body.

Body Condition

The Siamese must be in top physical condition with clear and alert eyes. It must be strong, lithe and muscular. It should neither be boney nor flabby nor should the Siamese be fat.

Body Color

Body

Its body color is to be even, it's shading subtle when allowed. For more mature cats, allowance should be given for darker color as the Siamese cat's color points generally darken as the feline grows older. However there must be a distinct contrast between color points and body color.

Color Points

The appearance of the mask, ears, legs, feet and tail is to be dense and stark in definition. The color points of the feline are to be well-defined and should share the same shade and color with the rest of the points.

Its mask is to cover the feline's entire face including its whisker pads and is joined to the ears by tracings. Mask is not to extend over the felines head nor there visible ticking or hairs of white in the points.

With Penalty

Off-color, spotted or otherwise labeled as improper shade or color of nose leather and/or paw pads.

Your cat will be penalized if its body is soft or mushy or has an obvious and visible protuberance at the end of the sternum cartilage under normal handling of the feline.

Disqualification Rules

If the cat is in poor health or any evidence of illness; has a hind leg that is weak or display weakness. If your cat is breathing through its mouth because of poor occlusion or nasal obstruction it is grounds for disqualification as well as emaciation or any visible kinks.

Eyes which are of a different shade and hue other than blue; toes and/or feet that is white in color. Has incorrect number of digits on fore and hind paws. A Siamese cat that has malocclusion resulting in either an overshot or undershot chin. Longhair.

Siamese Colors

Seal Point

Body is to display an even pale fawn to cream. It should be warm in tone or shading gradually into a lighter color on the chest and stomach. Points are a deep seal brown. Its nose leather and pads of the paws should share the same color as the color points and not vary in hue. Its eyes should be a vivid, deep blue color.

Chocolate Point

The body color of the Siamese is to be displayed as ivory with sans any shading. Points are to be visibly displayed as milk-chocolate colored and warm in tone. Its nose leather and paw pads should show as cinnamon-pink and its eye color must be a deep, vivid color of blue.

Blue Point

The body color of the Siamese is to be displayed as bluish white, is to be cold in tone and shading gradually to white on the chest and stomach. Color points are deep blue. Its nose leather and paw pads should show as the color of slate and its eye color must be a deep, vivid color of blue.

Lilac Point

The body color of a lilac point Siamese is to be displayed as glacial white with no apparent shading of any sort. Color points are a frosty grey with a pinkish tone. Its nose leather and paw pads should show as lavender-pink and its eye color must be a deep, vivid color of blue.

There is no allowance for outcross breeds.

The Thai Cat - TICA Standard

As for the Thai cat, the TICA breed standards requires that the Thai cat sport modified wedge-shaped head of medium width; it is to have rounded cheeks and its muzzle is to trail off to a rounded end - its face almost resembling a small garden spade which is tapered at the end.

Its head is to be longer than it is wide but never to an extremely visible degree. The eyes of the Thai cat are to display a full almond shape. Its ears must be a moderate medium or a tad larger in size with the tips sticking outward at a gentle angle.

Its gracefully lithe physique is to be moderately long but not in any way tubular. Legs of medium length are graceful when at rest or moving and are carried by medium-sized paws that are oval in shape. Its tail is to be the length of the cat's torso and tapers at the tip. Its coat is ideally short, soft and silky highlighting a pale, off-white color and thick, even point colors.

TCA Approved Siamese Cats

The Traditional Cat Association (TCA) recognizes that there are two types of Siamese cats.

One is the Classic sort and the other is the Traditional kind which the association (TCA) describes to be different from the modern day Siamese cats recognized and accepted today by the TICA, CFA and numerous other cat associations all around the world.

The Traditional Cat Association (TCA) illustrates that a Traditional Siamese cat has a head with a much rounder shape than its classic Siamese counterpart. The Traditional Siamese cat is big boned and has a visibly rounded body.

The Classic Siamese of the Traditional Cat Association is big-boned as well but sports a slightly longer body than the Traditional Siamese and it has a wide, wedge-shaped head. The Classic Siamese felines come in albino, as well as the same four-colour variety which has been given the stamp of approval by the CFA.

Chapter Eight: Breeding Your Siamese Cats

If you are interested in breeding your Siamese cat, this chapter will give you a wealth of information about the processes and phases of its breeding and you will also learn how to properly breed them on your own. You will also be given some grooming care tips so that you can ensure that your Siamese is clean, neat and presentable.

Siamese Cat Breeding Information

In general, cats have an estrous, or heat cycle. The queen (female cats) can enter her first heat or sexual maturity as young as 4 months, and she generally has 2 or 3 heat cycles during the breeding season, which usually occurs around February to October in the northern hemisphere. Female cats are induced ovulatory which basically means that they do not ovulate unless they are bred. This greatly increases the chances of conception when bred.

There are many signs that the queen is undergoing its heat cycle such as rolling, rubbing against objects, and kneading her back feet, and yowl repeatedly and loudly. If you notice your Siamese is doing this that means that she is ready for mating. This behavior typically last around 15 to 20 days and can repeat in more than 30 days if the queen is not bred. If the queen is bred, the cycle ends as her body prepares for pregnancy.

In the feline world, pregnancy is called gestation. Gestation lasts for about 60 to 63 days or within 2 months for most cats including the Siamese cat.

Its average litter size is about 6 kittens. Queens can be bred by more than one male during a heat period, the semen of male cats can stay inside the queen for a period of time even if the queen or female cat have already mated with other male cats, resulting in kittens from the same litter with different fathers. During the later stages of pregnancy, the queen seeks a nesting area and places bedding in a quiet, secluded spot. Make sure to provide your cat with a comfortable bed, feed it properly and don't disturb it as much as you can, so that it can produce healthy offspring.

Queen or female cats will repeatedly call a tom cat (male cat) when she is ready to mate with him. Another sign is that the queen sprays during their heat cycle to spread the smell of their readiness for mating. Once a tom cat sniffs it, he will stay and linger around the queen until mating happens. Male cats also respond to the queen in certain voice that is a call for mating. Whenever a queen will hear this call, she would run towards it. This whole communication or invitation of cats for mating is highly dependent on calling by these specific sounds.

The mating may last for about 5 - 10 minutes or even more. You will know that the mating is over, if the queen shrieks out loud. Once done, the female cat would do it again if she is ready, as long as she is still in her heat cycle; otherwise, she won't entertain or pay attention in any tom cat after the cycle was finished.

Usually a queen would keep on licking herself and gets ready for another mating session. The interval between mating sessions could be around 30 minutes or even few hours. It is also not necessary that a female cat would go back to the same tom cat next day. As mentioned earlier, this could result in producing kittens with multiple fathers.

During labor, time between contractions decreases typically around 2 to 3 minutes apart. The first kitten to be born takes about 30 minutes to 1 hour after strong contractions and the birth interval between kittens is usually 15 minutes to 30 minutes.

Upon giving birth the kitten is inside a placenta and wrapped in the amniotic sac membranes that will cover its muzzle. The mother cat should break these by licking to enable the kitten to breath.

The mother cat will also chew through the cord and eat the placenta, which is normal and nutritionally valuable for her, although quite gross for us humans. But before helping during the labor process, consult your veterinarian first or study and ask breeders on how to do this properly.

If you want to help in giving birth to your pet, make sure you have the following:

- Watch or clock
- Clean cloth or toweling face
- Small box
- Polar fleece, baby blanket etc. and hot water bottle
- Gloves
- Fresh bedding
- Scissors

Grooming Care

The coat of the Siamese cat is short and fine and will not require a lot of fussy maintenance when you groom it. The Siamese is a feline that is easy to care for given its close-to-the-skin fur. Give the Siamese coat a good, weekly combing to help evenly distribute essential oils and promote healthy skin. Regular brushing will also help eliminate shedding.

Scheduled brushing of its coat will likewise help stimulate its skin that in turn will promote a shinier coat free of knobs and knots. Doing so guarantees that your Siamese will maintain a softer, smoother coat all over.

Brushing your Siamese cat's teeth is a grooming requirement, as with all other domesticated pets living with human guardians, which promote overall wellness. Regular brushing of your Siamese cats' teeth ensures the feline a healthy head of champers and aids in the prevention of periodontal disease. Feline periodontal disease can lead to more serious conditions for your Siamese cat and can be totally avoided with routine diligence.

Chapter Nine: Keeping Your Siamese Cat Healthy

No matter whether pedigreed or of mixed-breed, Siamese cats experience varying incidences of health conditions and medical problems which may be of a genetic nature. Medical problems that could affect the health and wellness of a Siamese cat include the following

- Amyloidosis is a disease that manifests itself when a kind of protein called the amyloid is deposited in its body organs, primarily in the liver of the Siamese cat.
- Asthma/bronchial disease
- congenital heart defects like aortic stenosis

As with any pet a guardian might be thinking of taking in, the Siamese cat will be prone to some conditions that you will want to be aware of.

Aside from doing your own research on the possible health conditions your Siamese buddy may contract, it is advisable to network with other Siamese guardians who can share best practices with you and give you helpful tips and experienced knowledge of what to expect and what to watch out for when you bring home your own Siamese.

There is a world of information about the health matters of the Siamese, medical conditions and illnesses that may hound your furry buddy. Don't be caught off-guard. Gather information that will serve you well and you be well prepared for any eventuality.

Your vet is another trustworthy source of medical information regarding your Siamese cat. Consult with a trusted and established vet to get the low-down on the health conditions to which a Siamese could be prone.

Health and Lifespan

According to information on Swedish insurance data which tracked and followed cats up to 12.5 years old, the Siamese and Siamese-derived breeds displayed a higher instance in its mortality rate compared to other feline breeds. The majority of Siamese deaths were noted to be largely due to neoplasms; the primary culprit being mammary tumors.

The Siamese group's median lifespan was between 10-12.5 years. 68% of Siamese and Siamese-derived felines lived a span of 10 years or a more whilst 42% lived to 12.5 or more years. The record holder of the world's oldest male cat went to the Siamese named Scooter, who at 30 years old enjoys life with his guardian in Texas.

The Siamese cat has a higher morbidity rate than most other feline breeds in the spectrum. They suffer higher risks of gastrointestinal and neoplastic problems.

On the upside, the risks of a Siamese cat contracting a feline lower urinary tract disease are relatively low.

Across the pond, in England, collected clinical data has revealed a much higher median of the Siamese cat in life expectancy. Data reports have recorded a lifespan of 14.2 years over there.

Crossed Eyes and Tail Kinks

The most prevalent kind of progressive retinal atrophy or PRA in felines, which includes the large group of Siamese-related breeds, is associated to a mutation of the rdAc-gene which a DNA-test can identify and determine.

A mutation in the tyrosinase results in abnormal neurological connections between the brain and the eyes of the feline. This manifests an abnormal uncrossed wiring of the optic chiasm.

Many of the early Siamese cats were cross-eyed to compensate for the abnormality. But just like kinked tails, the incidence of crossed eyes were tagged as a flaw and through thoughtful, selective breeding this trait is seen far less and is not as common today as it was before.

The lack of tapetum lucidum causes reduced and compromised vision for the cat, even if its eyes are not crossed. This trait, which affects their hunting abilities during the night, is what paved the way for Siamese cats to become more inclined toward human companionship and be largely dependent on their caregivers.

This trait makes the Siamese cat more vulnerable to dangers in an urban setting like night-time road activity and motorway traffic. Siamese cats are great listeners unlike most other blue-eyed white cats who can be prone to reduced hearing ability.

The Siamese feline, above all most feline breeds and more notably during kitten hood, can be highly susceptible to infections of the lungs. It is also more frequently prone to Vestibular Disease, Feline Hyperesthesia Syndrome as well as Feline OCD than other feline breeds.

Siamese Cat Care Sheet

You have come to the end of this book. By now it is hoped that this book has shed clearer light and has allowed you a closer look and got to know the sweet Siamese cat a little more. Now that you've learnt what it would take for you as caregiver to be guardian of a Siamese cat we hope you have come closer to making a decision of taking in or buying a Siamese cat.

We hope this book which was aimed to enlighten you, the reader, of what to expect when considering a

Siamese cat has done just that. We encourage you to do further research and ask experienced guardians, neighborhood vets and registered breeders of good repute more about the Siamese cat. Another good thing about networking with other Siamese cat guardians is the precious exchange of best practices.

Keep in mind however that each cat no matter what pedigree or breed has its own distinct traits, characteristics, personality and behavior. What may be good for one may not necessarily be good for another. Remember that time will play a part in you and your Siamese cat getting to know each other.

The last chapter of this book gives you an overview of the things you need to remember and apply when you and your household collectively decide to become caregivers and guardians to your very own Siamese cat.

Here is a quick, last once over of important information to take away. We hope that you enjoy many days of warm cuddling and endless joy as you bring home your very own amiably docile, cuddly, fun and elegant - looking Siamese cat.

Basic Siamese Cat Information

Pedigree: Cat Fanciers' Association

Group: Siamese Cat

Breed Size: Medium,

Height: 10-15 inches (25-38 cm) tall

Weight: 8-12 lbs. for females and 8 lbs. for males

Coat Texture: short

Color: **Lilac point**, a glacial white body with frosty pinky-gray points and lavender-pink nose leather and paw pads; **Blue point**, a bluish-white body with deep blue points and slate-colored nose leather and paw pads; **Chocolate point**, an ivory body with milk chocolate-colored points and cinnamon-pink nose leather and paw pads; and **Seal Point**, a pale fawn to cream body with deep seal brown points and deep brown nose leather and paw pads

Eyes: expressively close-set almond-shaped eyes that are a vivid, deep blue.

Ears: set at a wide base the Siamese ears are big and sticks up from the sides of its head and forms an imaginary triangular shape.

Tail: its tail, long and thin, bearing the color point of the cat, tapers to an elegant point.

Temperament: it needs lots of attention, is a vocal chatterbox and loves being around and interacting with its caregivers.

Strangers: it is a sociable feline; hence, it is strongly advised that you keep your Siamese as an indoor pet to fend of cat-nappers.

Other Pets: with the guardians patient integration it easily adapts to other feline friendly pets you may own

Training: is very trainable and easily adapts to humans who handle them with care

Exercise Needs: lively and frequent exercise is highly encouraged for the Siamese cat to keep it agile and limber.

Health Conditions: Siamese cats are prone to Amyloidosis, asthma and aortic stenosis.

Lifespan: typical average lifespan is 11-15 years

Basic Nutritional Information

Nutritional Needs - diet rich in meats (chicken, pork or beef), commercial cat food, raw meat

Water Consumption - frequent replenishment of water dish is advised

Feeding Amount - varies on specific factors like history, gender, weight, size, age.

Feeding Frequency - It is best to consult with your vet about the amount of food you put out for your cat

Breeding Information

Heat period- two to three weeks

Sexual Maturity – 5 - 12 months

Female Breeding Age - 14 months

Male Breeding Age - 16 months

Litter Size - 6 kittens or more

Birth Interval - 15 – 30 minutes

Pregnancy- 60 - 63 days

Index

A

amino acid 8
antibodies 10

B

body 9, 10, 11
breed 8, 10, 11, 12, 13
breeder 7, 9
breeding 8, 10, 11, 12

C

Cat Fanciers Association 9
cattery 7
CFA 9
claw 10
coat 7, 8, 9, 11, 14
color 8, 9, 11, 13, 14
cycle 10

D

desexed 8, 14
diet 8
DNA 12
domestic 11

E

ears 9, 13
essential 8
estrus 8

F

face 9, 12, 13
family 11, 13
feet.. 12
female 8, 10, 11, 13, 14
fertile.. 10
food.. 11
fur 12, 13

G

genetic 7

I

infection 7
intact 13, 14

J

judge 7

K

kittens 11

L

lactating 10

M

male 8, 9, 12, 14
markings..7, 8, 11, 12, 13
milk 10
mite... 7
mutation 7

N

neutered 8
nose 12, 13
nutrients... 10

O

offspring 8, 10

P

pattern 7, 9, 14
pedigree 9, 11
pigmentation... 7, 9
protein 8
purebred 13

S

show.. 7, 12
skin...7, 12, 13

standard 8, 10, 13

T

tail 9, 13
traits 13

Photo Credits

Page 1 Photo by webandi via Pixabay.com,
https://pixabay.com/en/cat-siamese-cat-fur-kitten-2124270/

Page 16 Photo by SaeKawaii via Pixabay.com,
https://pixabay.com/en/siamese-blue-eyes-cute-feline-468814/

Page 31 Photo by rihaij via Pixabay.com,
https://pixabay.com/en/cat-mieze-siam-breed-cat-siamese-1724812/

Page 40 Photo by TaniaVdB via Pixabay.com,
https://pixabay.com/en/siamese-cat-cat-kitten-cat-baby-408746/

Page 60 Photo by Kapa65 via Pixabay.com,
https://pixabay.com/en/cat-domestic-cat-pet-cat-s-eyes-1711396/

Page 72 Photo by rihaij via Pixabay.com,
https://pixabay.com/en/cat-mieze-kitten-siamese-cat-siam-1648716/

Page 78 Photo by cornelazar via Pixabay.com,
https://pixabay.com/en/cat-siamese-breed-pet-portrait-1870974/

Page 98 Photo by liliy2025 via Pixabay.com,
https://pixabay.com/en/thai-cat-mother-pet-elegant-1710123/

Page 105 Photo by TaniaVdB via Pixabay.com, https://pixabay.com/en/cat-kitten-siamese-cat-cozy-202071/

Page 112 Photo by jwskks5786 via Pixabay.com, https://pixabay.com/en/cat-siamese-kitty-pet-animal-cute-2127782/

References

Siamese Cat - Cattime.com
<http://cattime.com/cat-breeds/siamese-cats>

Cat Proofing Your House - Wikipedia
<https://en.wikipedia.org/wiki/Siamese_cat>

**Siamese Cat Information and Personality Traits –
Hillspet.com**
<http://www.hillspet.com/en/us/cat-breeds/siamese>

Siamese Cat – Petmd.com
<http://www.petmd.com/cat/breeds/c_ct_siamese>

**The Siamese Cat Personality – Cats with Altitude!
Life – with – Siamese – Cats.com**
<http://www.life-with-siamese-cats.com/siamese-cat-
personality.html>

About the Siamese – CFA.org
<http://cfa.org/Breeds/BreedsSthruT/Siamese.aspx>

Siamese Breed Standard – CFA.org
<http://cfa.org/Portals/0/documents/breeds/standards/siame
se.pdf>

Cat Breed Profile: Siamese – Petful.com

<http://www.petful.com/cat-breeds/siamese-cat-breed-profile/>

Siamese vs. Thai – Petbreeds.com

<http://cats.petbreeds.com/compare/31-48/Siamese-vs-Thai>

The Original Thai Cat – The Thai Cat Center

<http://www.thethaicatcenter.com/>

Personality – The Thai Cat Center

<http://www.thethaicatcenter.com/the-maew-boran-personality.html>

Thai – TICA.org

<http://www.tica.org/find-a-breeder/item/287-thai-introduction >

About the Siamese Breed - Siamesebc.org

<http://www.siamesebc.org/aboutSiamese.shtml>

30 year old Siamese Cat is Named World's Oldest Living Cat – Foxnews.com

<http://www.foxnews.com/science/2016/05/10/30-year-old-siamese-cat-is-named-worlds-oldest-living-cat.html >

Is it Normal for a Siamese Cat to be Cross – Eyed -
Thenest.com
<http://pets.thenest.com/normal-siamese-cat-crosseyed-
8836.html>

Cats really are NICE: Felines prefer spending time with
humans over getting food, scientists claim
- Dailymail.co.uk
<http://www.dailymail.co.uk/sciencetech/article-
4353890/Cats-prefer-spending-time-humans-eating-
food.html>

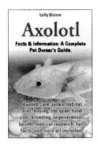

Feeding Baby
Cynthia Cherry
978-1941070000

Axolotl
Lolly Brown
978-0989658430

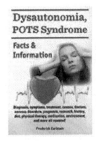

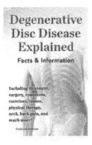

Dysautonomia, POTS
Syndrome
Frederick Earlstein
978-0989658485

Degenerative Disc
Disease Explained
Frederick Earlstein
978-0989658485

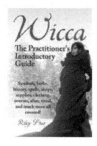

Sinusitis, Hay Fever,
Allergic Rhinitis Explained
Frederick Earlstein
978-1941070024

Wicca
Riley Star
978-1941070130

Zombie Apocalypse
Rex Cutty
978-1941070154

Capybara
Lolly Brown
978-1941070062

Eels As Pets
Lolly Brown
978-1941070167

Scabies and Lice Explained
Frederick Earlstein
978-1941070017

Saltwater Fish As Pets
Lolly Brown
978-0989658461

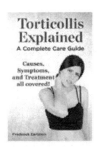

Torticollis Explained
Frederick Earlstein
978-1941070055

Kennel Cough
Lolly Brown
978-0989658409

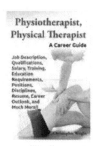

Physiotherapist, Physical
Therapist
Christopher Wright
978-0989658492

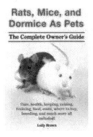

Rats, Mice, and Dormice
As Pets
Lolly Brown
978-1941070079

Wallaby and Wallaroo Care
Lolly Brown
978-1941070031

Bodybuilding Supplements
Explained
Jon Shelton
978-1941070239

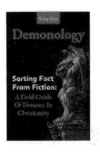

Demonology
Riley Star
978-19401070314

Pigeon Racing
Lolly Brown
978-1941070307

Dwarf Hamster
Lolly Brown
978-1941070390

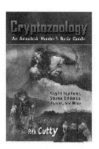

Cryptozoology
Rex Cutty
978-1941070406

Eye Strain
Frederick Earlstein
978-1941070369

Inez The Miniature Elephant
Asher Ray
978-1941070353

Vampire Apocalypse
Rex Cutty
978-1941070321

Made in the USA
Middletown, DE
18 June 2019